"'My first prophecy was a poem,' writes Liz Worth, conjuring the self in a state where the past portends an uncertain future. At this crossroads, personal experience informs universal truth, and *Inside Every Dream, a Raging Sea* unfolds like a spell cast to blur the line between legerdemain and the slow burn of daily life. A haunting, illusory read."

—Jim Johnstone, author of *The King of Terrors*

"Don't mess with the Old Magic if you aren't willing to face your own shadow. The poems in Liz Worth's poignant new collection, *Inside Every Dream, a Raging Sea*, do the real work of closely observing the discomfort that arrives in the aftermath of desire. The voice of these poems speaks as both gardener and guardian— it *tends to*, it *fends off*. 'Just imagine me as a woman / in a white dress, lightning in her hair.' Vulnerable, honest, steely, and steeped in a medicine made from bitter herbs, these poems are a reminder that every dream, if fully followed, eventually leads into a conversation with death. These meditations on loss and regret transform through their very refusal to look away or to contort into false promise. At the end of the spell, the voice returns to the earth and a pale bloom opens in its wake."

—Damian Rogers, author of *An Alphabet for Joanna*

"*Inside Every Dream, a Raging Sea* is a haunted house, a hurricane, a rotting tree. These poems feel ancient and elemental, almost like words we shouldn't be reading but can't walk away from. Beware of the spell they weave...and the ghosts that follow."

—Stephanie M. Wytovich, author of *On the Subject of Blackberries*

PRAISE FOR
The Truth Is Told Better This Way

"Liz Worth's second collection of poems is the site of different magics working themselves out."
—*Contemporary Verse 2*

"Worth's book is full of poems that will punch you in the gut, and twist your organs until they bleed out... A must read."
—*Luna Luna Magazine*

"*The Truth Is Told Better This Way* by Liz Worth is a book of piercing poetry that reads like a very intimate confession."
—*This Magazine*

PRAISE FOR
No Work Finished Here: Rewriting Andy Warhol

"What if you tore apart the city's tenderloin; if you seized its ephemera and—before burning all the sweet voodoo—collected the best and most brilliant cuts? This is Liz Worth's stylish master nightmare, *No Work Finished Here*."
—Lynn Crosbie, author of *Where Did You Sleep Last Night*

"Warhol would be the first to say, in his wrinkly voice, how excited he was that Liz Worth had done this to his novel. He might have even said something clever like, 'It should have just been poetry all along.'"
—*SubTerrain Magazine*

"Saying wow isn't saying enough... *No Work Finished Here* gains immediate entry into that lovely pantheon of absolutely essential Canadian poetry classics."
—*Today's Book of Poetry*

Inside Every Dream, a Raging Sea

Liz Worth

Inside Dream, Raging

Book*hug Press
Toronto 2024

Every

a

Sea

Liz Worth

Library and Archives Canada Cataloguing in Publication

Title: Inside every dream, a raging sea / Liz Worth.
Names: Worth, Liz, 1982– author.
Identifiers: Canadiana (print) 20240345576
Canadiana (ebook) 20240345584
  ISBN 9781771669092 (softcover)
  ISBN 9781771669238 (EPUB)
Subjects: LCGFT: Poetry.
Classification: LCC PS8645.O767 I57 2024
DDC C811/.6—dc23t

The production of this book was made possible through the generous
assistance of the Canada Council for the Arts and the Ontario Arts Council.
Book*hug Press also acknowledges the support of the Government
of Canada through the Canada Book Fund and the Government of
Ontario through the Ontario Book Publishing Tax Credit and the Ontario
Book Fund.

 Canada Council Conseil des arts
for the Arts du Canada
 ONTARIO ARTS COUNCIL
CONSEIL DES ARTS DE L'ONTARIO
an Ontario government agency
un organisme du gouvernement de l'Ontario
 Ontario

 Canadian Patrimoine Canada
Heritage canadien
 ONTARIO
CREATES

Book*hug Press acknowledges that the land on which we operate is
the traditional territory of many nations, including the Mississaugas of
the Credit, the Anishnabeg, the Chippewa, the Haudenosaunee, and the
Wendat peoples. We recognize the enduring presence of many diverse
First Nations, Inuit, and Métis peoples, and are grateful for the opportunity
to meet and work on this territory.

Book*hug Press

Contents

Inside Every Dream, a Raging Sea

ꟾ Don't Want It Like I Used To

1.

I find you gasping at my front door, expecting to come in. Can't you see the mess that's already been made? You expect me to clean up after you, too? You want to go digging up old magic, that's your business. It'll be your problem when you don't like what you find. You know I sweep these steps for a reason, but these seeds still manage to find ways to take root.

There are so many things I never wanted to give life to. Too much has already grown from this house.

2.

Shut your mouth: That spell hasn't worked in a long time. Those memories? Pale wishes.

You used to think you could do it alone. And for a while, you did.

Isolation erodes all meaning. You weren't sure whether you were living your own reality anymore, or lost in someone else's. You needed to come back home.

Look at you now. The scorch of your movements, the fluidity of your gaze. When will you tell me where you've been?

3.

Let me show you the true shape of my mouth, its curves and circles.

I don't dream like I used to. I can't picture when it all stopped. Probably around the same time I started to wonder if other people's lives were like mine: piles of paper scattered around the house, drawers that could never be cleared out, hours dwindling to bare threads.

A blister on the inside of my foot, a monument to the time I've wasted.

Once, I touched my finger to my knee and a thousand tiny moons spilled out around my ankles.

When was the last time you saw me in the daylight? Sorry, I shouldn't ask questions like that. My words don't work the way they once did. I could have been imitating wolves instead of performing so many emotions, but now it's too late.

My body never should have bent like that. Contorting to fit into places I never wanted to be in.

See there, where the bruise won't heal? I can't keep my finger out of there no matter how much it hurts. But when I close my eyes, I see flowers, great flourishes of red and purple and, just for a second, I almost start to dream.

Other Half

What are these photographs you've left me with:
your thumb in the wrinkle near my mouth,
a new understanding of what my frame can hold.

The way I saw myself, later:
thick with deception,
aged from wear.
I was never what you thought I was.
Still, you slept here,
left an unfinished story
beneath my feet.

Look, I shouldn't have been doing all of this with
wet hands, too much to hold on to.
And now it's all slipped away.

Walls take their time to talk.
If I sit here long enough maybe
I will finally learn that not everything
has to be said at once.

And when it was my turn to speak, oh:
so many lies have come out of me.
Enough of a web to be woven into something new.
Every strand, spun into the shape of another woman.

She looks just like me, lives the life I once had.
She's always hungry; I feed her constantly.
You probably heard her in the kitchen after you went to bed.
We've both got you fooled, impossible to tell us apart, the way she
laughs at the right times and stays so busy.
You don't notice I'm not even here anymore.

I made myself so small
to sustain this other life but
I'd started disappearing long before she ever arrived.
I'd lent myself out to other fictions,
didn't know how thin it would make me.

Every day I lose a few more of my verses.
I don't write like I used to.
I can't get back to the way things were.
I can't fit into my old shape, I'm just enough
to thread myself through the needle that sews me shut:
cross my heart and hope to die.

Fear is a false food that burns more than it gives.
I watch for faces I wish weren't familiar.

Unravel these threads, the knots in the back of my hair.
Help me dry my hands. Show me that they have been washed
    enough
and that something can still be mine.

Not Everything at Once

What did you learn of my life, reading too much into the coffee
stains on my papers, patterns of dust on the bathroom mirror.

Every night I close my eyes and let the sun's last hour burn the day
off my lids.

We used to wander for hours on Sundays.

Around here the streets have no sidewalks. People look at me
from their car windows as though I'm breaking a rule.
I have six words written on the first page of a notebook. I can't take
them further than that.

In my kitchen, I bend spoons, take inventory of what's already been
used, the parts of me that once had a tale to tell.
I didn't come all this way to write books my mother would like. At
least empty cupboards are easy to entertain.

You were the one who wanted a strange future. But that wish was
the wrong spell. I knew it the second you said it. We were outside
the supermarket. As the statement left your mouth an old woman
lifted her finger to the sky, clutching a rock to her chest with the
other hand. Her grip crushed it to sand.

I have since learned to relax, arms settled at my sides, eyes easily
lost in thrift-store portraits of faded grins.

Sometimes I think that my tongue is a bone that *clack-clack-clacks*
the questions I'd rather not ask.

You understand now why I wouldn't take your call. If I sit here long
enough this place will finally tell me something.

I still wear the silver necklace you gave me. It looks different, too, its delicate chain flawed with the bloom of tarnish.

Do I still sound the same, at least?

Places like this aren't what you think they are. Up close the white vinyl siding is always stained with dirt. The grass is thin; you can see the earth between the blades. The whir of the bus route three blocks away is enough to wake you just as you're falling asleep.

What is it that you couldn't find? Does this feeling ever leave, the one that says there must be more, always more than this?

Anticipation

Three winds rise up these hills. Can you feel the difference
between them?

I can, but only if I close my eyes and listen—hard—to the hum of
the sun.

Trees used to grow here. See? Their stumps are nearly buried
under all this grass.

Give me a taste of something I had once. The flesh of a peach
in August, the juice on my chin. I used to hate the stickiness of
anything on my face.

I walked all night once just to see what might happen. The birds
sang themselves awake. Someone held my hand and I thought
Please don't let this end, but dawn isn't known for keeping
promises.

Not that I kept very many myself. Turns out none of us do. But to
admit it means losing the hope of having anything to look forward
to.

There comes a time when it gets harder to be excited for the
future. You look too young to know such things, though. You
shouldn't be here yet. It's too early.

Go. Forget what I told you about those winds. There's nothing to
hear in them, nothing more to look for than your own sense of
time.

Maybe, Sometimes

I read your letter. Twice.
It was full of sand and grated the tips of my fingers.

A poem came to my throat,
tasting of pale petals.
I swallowed it carefully. Later,
it blossomed into the unexpected,
a birth I never wanted.

Tonight, the sky is a colour it has
never shown me before.
I want to reach out, take hold of
its clouds. But I dare not:
look at these hands,
the messes they make.

I'm not who I'd planned to be.
Maybe that's what ghosts are:
rejections, unmet expectations.

Thunderclap, my pulse
a wave against rock.
A sore inside my cheek
where certain pleas have become ingrown.
I still worry about
the same things I always did:
sore throats and early appointments,
running out of time.

What shape would I take
if I were thrust into the sky?
I am not a crescent moon.
There are too many things within
that I can't satisfy.

Do you think maybe, sometimes,
you could hang a purple scarf over your lamp?
Leave the curtains open.
I will stand on the sidewalk.
You don't even have to come out.
Just imagine me as a woman
in a white dress, lightning in her hair.

Not Like Yours

Laughter has never seemed so far away until now. The surface of this world is a skin pulled tight across my head. Try to stand any taller and I'm crowded by spaces I'm no longer invited into. The only way out is down, but how deep do these fissures run and what if I don't have enough breath to make it through?

I can't tell you how long it's been since I last dared to look at my own face. I know I'm older now; I can tell by the tremors my hands have become. Every day I make up my eyes, my lips. I see the shadows of who I was left on my pillowcase each morning. I paint overtop, let it build, the one routine that keeps me going.

Kill the light. I don't need it anymore; these candles are enough. Can't you see? There's no sense in being able to look at everything so closely now. I've learned all I need to through the thin lick of flame, tapered wax drips to keep time with the hours that pass. Different from the ones you know, my days are not like yours.

Spells of the Twenty-First Century

Kiss me like you mean it. I've been waiting to know the power of your delirium, reckless ecstasy at all hours. The way you stand on the corner every weekend and let the whole world run through you. Poison voices, copper pennies. I could survive off your thoughts alone.

You paint your eyes thick to put the city in a haze, wait to be asked what temple you rose from. The magic you work is not from around here. Don't tell me where you learned it.

I want you to touch me, though I'm afraid you'll reach my head full of nothing but questions, my hands always wanting.

You always say you'll come to see me again tomorrow. I never trust you. You are wilder than me, not made to know time the way I do, not bound by expectations.

Leave me. This garden is mine, see what I grow for you. Spells of the twenty-first century and deep gazes that are just beginning to bud.

Seafoam

The final migration of the lie happened on the highway.
Cocteau Twins on the stereo, sand on the dashboard.
The word dissolved into seafoam the moment it was born.

You were not wrong to call this a miracle.

We pulled over after ten miles. In the back of the corner store,
two women were talking, louder than necessary:
You know the Devil's been around here again.

You choked on the air, flavoured with sweat.

The dead take care of those who remember them.
Lately, I've been wondering: who will remember me?
I've no one to leave behind.

From the highway, we could see all the places
where the original ancestors
asked the moon to reveal its mysteries.

Yet when I tried to speak to Her,
the moon became an angry mirror:
Remove your lips from mine.

It's what I should have told you to do when you burned a hole
in my black stockings, tried to convince me it was my style:
You like the attention.

Call down the constellation of shame, eat it with your bare hands.
You'll clean the dirt from under your nails.
Eventually, you get used to the filth.

This is the cost of memory:
screaming into an empty room. My teeth are growing teeth.
I stuff my mouth with hair, fingernails,
the tension of 4:00 a.m. that rises
in waves of heat across the skin.

My impatience, a useless ocean.

This was the invention: you said you weren't there when it
happened.
But I have a stain on the front of my dress,
and anyone would recognize the shape of your hand.

Denial. It's why you wanted to drive so far.
Because these streets record
the pace of my steps, absorb every plot line.

Don't you know how gravity works?

We walk the Earth, but it also walks us,
every step a reclamation,
pulling us back where we belong.

Summoning Spirits

Come closer: let me breathe onto the side of your face so you can feel the weight of all I still hold. These demands, a spring uncoiling.

No one ever tells you it's not about what you're heading for so much as what you're leaving behind.

But what choice was mine?

I had done things a woman wasn't supposed to do: left makeup stains on a stranger's lapel, spoke too loudly with the swing of my hips. Walked everywhere alone, muttering crooked charms my grandmother had knotted around my tongue. Watched as these words ran loose through the neighbourhood.

Secrets stay wherever they land and all of mine were buried right within my gut. I carried them across the water and not even the ocean that gave me sickness could drag up what I'd swallowed. Whole years went by and I stayed quiet.

Never sent letters home. Best to be forgotten.

I had enough to fathom as it was.

How are you, now? I wonder, sometimes, whether you've roused sympathy with the depths of the sea or sky.

Memory of Place

I write this from the edge of my teeth.

It's always quiet in here, the kind of room that listens. Run your tongue along its eastern side to taste all it has taken in.

I can still catch a hint of you, the spoil in your queries on your last day here. An aftertaste of sour milk.

The woman next door died three nights after you left. You remember how she used to knock on the wall when the TV was too loud. After I heard the news, I lay in bed and knocked back, just to say goodbye. I swear she answered me: *tick-tick-tock.*

One-Mississippi-two-Mississippi-three-Mississippi-four: counting down the rainstorm on a Sunday night, one of your favourite things to do. You always liked connections that couldn't be replicated, always longed for moments we could never plan.

What are you doing now, still staying up too late writing down plans you haven't yet made? Still eating apples whole, core and seeds even, over the kitchen sink?

Do you ever remember me the way I remember you? I know there are a lot of things I've forgotten—you always reminded me when I let something slip my mind. But I do think of you, the way your bare feet brushed these floorboards, the crackle of static in the sheets in mid-winter.

You can come home any time. Everything we had is still here.

Afterimage

I close my eyes for the last time
and wake up at the coffee shop.
You spill sugar packets across the table,
look for patterns of future histories. Draw spirals,
symbols of memories we may not live through.

I hold twenty colours.
You're hungry for all of them.
Our voices rise until every word twists
into a thin white rope that hangs above the table.

A woman two seats over hushes:
Try not to speak of the worst you've seen.
Each syllable is a hammer that leaves an
afterimage of strain.

It starts to rain.
I try to count the drops on the window
before they blur together.

If ever I am an old man,
let me wear a black hat over long hair.
The only sacrament I could carry out
when my delusions are as old as river rocks.

You're already ahead of me,
skipping time because you're afraid
of what it will do to you.

The woman at the next table speaks again,
louder this time:
God's eye sets everything ablaze.
I burn my mouth on a sip of coffee and
weep for all we are.

Seven Seeds

An old man came up to me on the street. His hair smelled of salt.
He told me Tuesdays were for raising hell, Fridays for receiving
grace.

Then he puckered his lips as though for a kiss and blew warm
breath against my forehead.

He told me he had put seven seeds inside of me.
They can grow to become anything you wish.

He told me to wash with cinnamon for seven days.
Cleanse yourself for the ritual.

He told me to wait for the first sign of pain to arrive.
It will come in the form of frost and the scent of regret.

Every night I bathed by candlelight. I let my hair stay heavy with
oils. As I slept, my tresses wove themselves into hands that
plucked feathers from my pillow.

On the seventh day I woke expecting dread. I watched the sky for
omens and tried to stay inside.
Nothing happened until late in the afternoon.

There was pain, but different than I thought: a fluttering cramp on
my right side, and then exactly ten hot tears, five from each eye.

The first thing that grew was a memory I thought I had thrown
away years ago: I won't tell you what. We all have at least one
souvenir like it, and I am sure you can imagine mine.

The second seed to sprout became a bent branch of lost time.
I needed it back except I didn't know what to use it for.

On the third day another seed broke open. This one was different
than the rest, turning black in places and sprouting fuzz. It grew
into a friendless year. I know what it's like to wait and have no one
come.

A temporary spirit arrived next. It was haunted by tortures and
begged for help: *Feed me with the glow of a match and a bowl of
dirty water.* I cast the spell and the spirit became a white mare.

The mare's hooves scattered the remaining seeds and I had to
hunt for them under the couch. One seed had broken apart and
I inhaled its contents. Could I be the Oracle of Delphi this way?
The seed offered nothing but dust, although later I laughed and
something came out of me: neediness and deceit, a part of myself
I always wanted to send away. Unspoken, it won't leave. Now it
spoils in the pantry.

On the sixth day a sound grew. It started as a distant humming
and then became a song. Some feelings are so deep they cannot
be surfaced through language, only music, or noise.

The final seed bore something that had gone missing long ago.
I only got a glimpse of her face as she left me: feral, a witchmother,
maybe. Fingers like roots, eyes the tides of a full moon. She ran as
soon as she was freed. Ran like she knew the moment was coming.

Black Annis

Trip on the sidewalk. Skinned knee, another crack in the shell.

I walk because I don't know what else to do.

My molars are black from untruths. Everything ends up in writing.

This house is blemished. There are places even the wind won't touch. And that patch of damp on the rug—it never dries. Nothing here stays mended. Signs of a curse, surely.

What would you say about your life if you only had four minutes to say it? Me, I would exorcise at least five years of reminiscence. Bodies buried in too many graves.

This should have been easier.

I called on Black Annis the witch to help me, lit a blue candle in Her name and made the hand gestures my grandmothers taught me. But not even She cares to grace this place.

What will have me, then?

Every corner around here is as worn as I am. What will hold me when I decide not to turn around?

It's Not as Bad as It Looks

You say *psychic* and I see a spectre.
It crawls out of the back of your shirt, hovers
over the dining-room table.
It stares at me. You pretend not to see it.

The food on my plate is cold,
leftover from yesterday.
I mash it into the ceramic.
White cream squeezes through
fork prongs.

There's still blood on my leg. Dirt
from a fall that afternoon.
Gravel in the wound.
It's not as bad as it looks.

A red stain on the carpet,
a spot in your vision.
A cut comes between us because you let it.

I'm hungry but can't eat for all the talking.
The answers you want don't exist.
Still, you press for omniscience, believing
there's more to me, believing everything
a pretense.

Every thought in your head belongs to me, you say,
Did you know that?

If you can see so much, why do you miss
the aversion of my eyes, the guilt in my speech?

Somewhere upstairs, something breaks.
We pretend not to hear it.

The oracles are tired. They tell me so when I go to bed.
Praying, I ask for something kinder than this.

The sheets are cool against my legs, backs of my calves still hot
from the late-spring sun.

Sleep reads me a story. Spirits pass through me.
My gullet overtaken in a friendly possession.
My identity a transmission.
Tuned to channels we don't watch at home.
Revealing a face I haven't yet worn.

The possibility of morning is never as true
as what it seems before I wake.

Still, I hold on to what I can.

The Ride Home Is Never Quick

Tonight on the train a woman holds fistfuls of trash. Balled-up papers and used tissues. She clutches them to her chest, treasures or children. Her eyeliner is an inch thick and running into the creases of her skin. She refuses to sit even though she was on the train before I got here and nearly every seat is empty.

I smile at her. She opens her mouth and a silver thread of spit leaks down her chin. It lands on the front of her black sweater, shines in the light. Her legs are bare, skin dry, flaking. Her shoes look expensive from a distance, but up close their heels are buckling and the leather is scuffed.

At the final stop, the driver tells everyone to get off. The woman shuffles ahead of me, but instead of heading for the exit she sits on the bench. Paper falls around her. She watches it all roll away and yells at something I can't see.

Down the street from here is where J and M got into a fight once. Broke beer bottles in the parking lot, aiming glass at each other's heads. I don't collect stories like that anymore, but I feel them constantly. My old friends are all ghosts that haunt every empty lot.

People around here say they have other types of ghosts—the ones that live in your house and breathe down your neck. The week my grandfather died, a white dog followed my grandma all the way home. It sat on the lawn and watched her go into the house. She never saw the dog again but always believed it was her Elmer come back to let her know he was checking on her.

I walk fast under the bridge, hurrying from one light to another. Everyone who walks alone around here gets followed home eventually.

I forgot to leave the light on for myself. My fingers get cold searching for my keys. I wonder: Do phantoms feel the cold like we do? Do they wish for gloves when the frost comes at night, and do they miss warm beds and porch lights?

April

When I was famished, I fed myself by digging
into the spaces between your songs.
I felt around for bones, found a covenant that tasted of cherries.

Tell me if you stayed up late or lived for mornings.
When the night called to you, what stars did you look for
when you read the sky?

What came through you as you sang?
Your tone a channel, the body a vessel.

Tell me how I am supposed to listen to the odes you wrote.
I wait for them to drift up from the street.
I reassure myself with every flutter of the curtains.

You'd shown me a spiral staircase in an old church,
held my hand as we walked its rounds.
It left me dizzy, heart strong beneath my T-shirt.
I go there now, feed from the iron rails.
I hum a melody you played only for me
and the sky breaks open.
The rain is a sorceress.
I let her into me, parched for attention.

Later, I whisper to myself as I walk home.
It's good. It's good. It's good, I say.
Do I sound convincing?

I dream of a touch so real it leaves an impression on the sheets.
Did you intend this, to be the one to live on in threads
woven out of dissonance? I try to induce you through
English rain and wool. You come in other ways,
playing tricks with the light.
Your grief is both yours and mine.

The grip grows a callous on my hands.

A Future Cut with Fires

Something's been watching me through the window. A god
of the woods, its mouth a slit, and on its head are horns
instead of hair. *It's no god,* you say. *Just a shadow.*
Still, I leave a black candle in the centre of the room.
Just in case.

There was a time I believed myself to be possessed,
sensing a demon by the smell
of blood left behind.
I thought the dark circles on the floor were from its claws.
Turns out, they were just burns on the tiles
where you'd nodded off with a cigarette.

See that corner there?
That's where I saw the ghost of the child I used to be.
She looked at me and asked, *Do you accept me?*

The shame of evocation, seeing yourself as you once were.
Carrying every crisis since between the folds of your coat.

Now I walk down the street, running
my hands over my hips, pulling power.
I stand in the middle of the road and
wait for a car to hit me.
I stare into you, cutting myself open,
and you don't even notice.

Do you ever see what I see?
Sacred geometry, the circles we cross.
A future cut with fires.

Let's get away for a while, you say.
I forget to pack anything that matters.
On the drive up north the road hums
its ambient desires.

In the cabin you give me something sour to drink.
We walk on the gravel road and all the trees have faces.
One points at me, brings its long, bony finger to my forehead.
The sun is still out when I fall asleep, and I convince myself
I made all of this up, that I've been lying the whole time.

My whole life, a myth.

What am I without the spirits I see dancing?

In the morning you urge me to touch the walls and windows.
Cool surfaces, nothing that can escape too soon. Oh, what
talismans these walls contain: light and wind,
time marked by weather.

I fully disintegrate,
rebuild from the gravel
that clogs your mouth.

Etymology

I was never looking in the right direction.
On the street with my head down, scavenging.
At home, eyes to the windows, or searching the wardrobe for
hidden exits, secret doors.

I found an entry point through a hole in your jeans. Back pockets
faded around the shape of a wallet, pyramids rising from the keys
in front. In your hand was a map written between knuckles and
whorls. I held on as tight as I could, deciphering lines and roads
through a clench that wouldn't let up.

You were the reason I left. I wanted to, but I also didn't.
I knew my mother would miss me. I didn't want my father
to think about the things I might be doing
so far out of reach.
You got the ride. Picked me up.
I pretended that I was on parade,
on a triumphal chariot, victor on the other side of a war.

I overlooked it when you didn't have the cash
to pay for the cab. The money was still warm
when the driver handed me my change.
Later, in your bedroom, with the lights off and TV on,
you told me of a story you wanted to write
about a girl who was so ugly she became beautiful.
So beautiful that she had to die young, be cursed
by everything she could not control.

You never wrote the story.
None of this matters because we're already dead,
you used to say whenever I asked you about it.
I didn't write much during those days, either. My head,
lost in hunger, and my eyes, searching again.

I don't know when it happened that my hand stopped
reaching for yours. I'd walked to the end of every road
and that map was no longer legible.

I didn't go home for weeks after I left. My mind
didn't work anymore, not like it used to, and the utterances
I needed to get back inside were gone.
Maybe you'd taken them, written them into one of your
notebooks and let them languish.
Language dies, too, you know. If we don't keep
our words alive, they leave.

I started wearing linen gowns to bed and
reading late into the night.
I bought daisies from the corner store and
set them up on a small table, the only
piece of furniture I had at first.
I formed new phrases by talking to myself and
built the dialect that I now speak.

Flesh From Bone

When you write, you call down the stars, pluck them from the sky. A different configuration every time. Your thumbs bleed. I want to kiss them, but you save it all for your journal: *The page is thirstier than we are.*

When you write, you tear flesh from bone. I find pieces of you scattered around the house later. Soul reduced to grit between your fingers. A grasp nothing can escape. Your head drowns and your legs carry you off into the night. You never tell me where you walk to, but you must go for miles, for hours.

When you write, you think of all the faces you don't see anymore. You play upon every scar and wrinkle. You prey upon your own, digging at the consonants that rest between your teeth, the apparitions caught in your eyes. You think of everything that was and could have been and when I ask, *Do you ever think of me?* You say that writing is not for lovely things.

I want to tell you that your writing is a ritual that lets too many things in. A portal that you never manage to close properly. I've seen what walks through the doors you leave open.

I feel selfish and alone. Jealous of all the things you would rather spend time with: manifestations of bad nights and whiskey hangovers. Muses to you, muzzles to me.

Time Keeper

Leave me at the side of your bed. It's time.

Your size undermines
the filaments of anger that hold you together.

You hid secret planets in your closet. Only let
me see them on odd days, a calendar I could
never follow. Your history keeps you red and taut,
every action woven through knotted limbs.

I have all the things that ever mattered to you:
an old note from your mother,
an orange cardigan worn thin at the elbows,
a brooch in the shape of a cat.
They are safe with me.
I keep them out of the sun.
The note is in the pocket of the sweater.
Its ink is fading, but slowly.
Every Sunday I read it aloud to keep it alive:
See you soon. XO

I can live with it all because you made it so.
If you want me to, I will wear something of yours
and think of you.
Maybe you would like to visit then.
You can slip in through the open window or
travel in on the sunlight that crosses the floor
each afternoon.

Red Offerings

Circle the street corner again.
Forbidden to know the same happiness
as everyone else.
There, a warm window. Yellow light
against the moon. Portrait of
someone else's living room,
someone else's life.

I empty the contents of my pockets,
leave them on a weak patch of grass.
This city is an altar, hungry to receive.
I give what I can.

Lines of poetry course through me
on my way home. My thoughts are
full of hexes but rarely do I find
direction for them. Paint myself
grey with diluted ideas, sick in
the mind yet no one can see it.

Help me feel a little danger on my breath.
My first prophecy was a poem:
what goes ignored grows.

Dew settles on the grass.
The cushion of humidity to
pass between the rages.

At home, I yell. My voice,
disproportionate to the
size of the room.
The furniture rearranges itself
in response.
My ankle catches on a leather boot
left astray on the rug.
I barely feel a thing.

I'm tired but I can't quiet myself
enough to sleep.
The volume of my logic buzzes.
The violence of routine.

No. The violence of desire.

Feel how much smaller I have
become since I gave up everything else.
Small enough to barely be here at all.

You Don't Know Me Like You Used To

Wake me up when you're wild. I like you coarse with animal secrets. The scent of a street I've never been down before. The perfume of a memorial I've yet to unearth.

All of my fantasies end when I lay my bare shoulder on cold pavement.

I stopped looking up at the sky and lost track of days. I had to turn away from the birds; they had started staring back at me. You taught me to know their portents. They sang of the moon's own obsessions for rotting silk and forgotten names, heralded threats under wingspans.

You plucked the Devil card from your tarot pack as an act of protection. Discarded it in the yard where it ended up in a robin's nest, criss-crossed by mud and twigs. Even in pieces the Devil enchanted, cuddled into down and quills, etching itself into whistles and chides.

This makes the moon laugh. I cover my ears when I hear birds in the bush. They flap their wings. Old incense and rot tinge the air.

Strange how the odd one still taps at the window some nights, calling back my attention. I keep the blinds drawn.

I've had revelations. The first was in a bad apartment after taking a peculiar pill. My existence hovered with its shoulder to the ceiling before pulling away like a snake. Every image new, a surprise even. What have I done with the mind I once cultivated?

I shouldn't ask you, though. Don't expect you to know me like you used to. Ever since we buried the bodies of your misconceptions in the yard last year. Their hard edges, soft curves. All the letters tangled together as we dug the hole deeper.

If I had to be a letter I'd be the letter *E*, as easy as smoke.

The last time we talked—really talked—you asked me what it's like to live so close to regret. At first, I used to scrub the baseboards every other night. Gave away my favourite things. Threw out my diaries. Eventually, though, I stopped thinking about it, settled into disgrace.

Private Light

February weather: in the private light
of a cold corner,
I ruin who I am. Again.
Send away a certain kind of shadow,
hoping it comes back to me
as clarity.

My uncle once told me that
when a dog
gets a taste
of blood,
it's never the same again.

I have desires that are no longer safe to nurture.
The way I walk along the lake at night, tempting
voices out of the tides.
The way I let men look at me,
always wanting more.

It takes me two hours
to leave the apartment.

The day's first ritual: I rest my head
on a pillow, worn flat in the middle.
Thirst for the cool surface of sleep,
horizon of quiet.

Later, I dress quickly, but can't
leave until every candle in the cupboard
is lit, then extinguished.
A ceremony of compulsion,
a spell only cast
on myself.

Outside, I bury an egg beneath a tree.
An older woman passes by,
tells me a saga that happened
in *year nineteen.*
She knew a different idol, then.
Something more merciful than what I worship now.

On my way home, it starts to rain.
There are things you learn, living in the city:
don't turn corners too sharply, for one.
Someone's always on the other side.

How soft our bellies are,
how defensive our appearances,
mine daring to be dirty.

What I once thought all women
would be like is not what I
have become. Dreaming
in gasps, I hide myself
within wet ground and
the crackle of lit candlewicks,
hungry and looking for
something I've yet to know.

Wasp

Overcast, the sky still
throws enough light
that I need to squint.

The pull of a satin sheet
across the thigh seems
louder than it should be.

How many names does
the body contain?
Maybe bones are recording devices,
brittle not through time
but the weight of documentation.

Play me a song before I have the chance
to change my mind.

You feed on lukewarm tea, toast.
There are crumbs around your mouth.
I'll eat from the plate the dog's been licking.

A raised voice floats through the window.
Foreshadowing, I assume.

You ask a question and I conjure
an image of a dead rat
eaten by wasps. I swear
I feel the sting.

There's nothing I can do
that is ever entirely
comfortable.

After I started spending time with you,
I started to see relief in things I
once ran from.

A dish clatters in the sink.
Rain hits the roof.
A knot has formed in my hair.
I tug at it, fingers hurried, rough.
Strands break.

It reminds me of a piece of
advice someone once gave me.
More like a warning, really,
about what happens when
you try to grab hold
of an open flame.

White Lace, Pale Lipstick

Copper daybreak.
Breath visible against the wind.
Wishing it weren't so early.
All of the appropriate drinking hours
take so long to arrive.

I used to undo myself wherever I went,
inviting unknown faces to sit with me,
my head a recess of humiliation.
Somewhere along the way
I must have decided to be strange. No:
something beyond that, even.
Disorienting myself through the
stream of a song: whose jinxes
keep me afloat? Vessel of
spent days, and it's starting
to show. You can see the
tired lines in my face.

You used to ask me
what I think about when I come.
Nothing, mostly.
Or at least not you.

Once, I thought of the edges
of a diamond.
If—*if*—my thoughts do form,
they run impatient: when
will this be over?

Imagine the power of living
as a random shout, the kind
that rises from street corners.

Sometimes, in those moments, I
have become a piece of
white lace or a shade of
pale lipstick.

Can't you see, now, why it's
getting so hard for me to stay here.

I love you differently than before.
I knew it the day I saw seven dead birds,
each on different streets.
I took one of them home to see if
I could find out what they know.
I plucked its feathers and
boiled it down to bones.
Drank the broth, waited for a message
to become clear:

Nothing here is alive anymore.

Hands

Let me rest my hands a moment.
They've been busy throwing shadows,
casting stories with the motions that
pull the right lore from my tendons.
Every syllable a witch, cackling.

When the coven starts to grow, I know
I've said enough.

Except here's the part I don't want
anyone to hear: God watches me through my window
at night. He's shown up three times this week.
I try not to look at him: he's nothing like you'd imagine.
Face like a rock, mouth a thin opening, always frowning.
Sometimes he seems as though he's about to speak but
I don't wait long enough to let him, shooing away his petitions
like flies. The power is in the wrists, see? The way they make
my pinkies flick and snap, bones built on the back of time.

The dead tell me that grief is strong enough to eat you alive.
If it's taking me, it can't be fast enough. All I feel is a slow
sickness in the pit of my gut, but it's nothing
a little wine can't cure.

I can't walk close enough to the truth. Not even poetry takes me
there.

I can barely supress what's inside.

Young Fox

Let me take you to the place in the woods where the forest is hungriest and all offerings are devoured.

The stronger the yearning, the faster the results. So, swallow me whole.

I found this place three winters ago, following a single pair of footprints in the snow. Boot size much larger than mine. The steps went in, but not back out. They ended at the river's edge, water flowing black with cold.

How easy it is to slip away, unseen.

The things I could show you, if you spent a little time on me. I'm older than I look. Nicer, too. I see colours when I eat and sometimes, just sometimes, I can hear another's thoughts before they're spoken.

Come. I'll hold you the way I was never held. Later, I'll open up the box I keep over there. Let you see things I don't easily speak of. Sometimes, it's best to wait until the mind is easier.

Your mind is a young fox, bounding over tall grass. Mine is cluttered with a song I heard twenty years ago. The notes ramble around, as alive as they were when first played. I often sing it when I walk down the street. In twenty years, I've felt all angles of the sun on my face and this music has played through each one.

Time is an imposter disguised as promise. I have inherited parts of my figure from people I will never know. How long does it take to find yourself?

I am the kind of person who regrets everything. I see how I could have done it all differently. I now hear a hesitancy in my proclamations that wasn't always there.

I wish I could spend a day in another person's form. Just to take a break from my own. Maybe you wish the same? If you did, you could try mine on, too. Then you'd know that the taste I maintain is ripe with metal. There's an old fork in my kitchen drawer that looks nothing like the others. I don't know where it came from, or how its prongs became so bent, its handle blackened with spots. I don't know when that fork became the only one I'll use.

If you light a purple candle for several nights in a row, you gain the ability to fly. I tried it once and no one saw me for three whole days.

I often think of a time I made my mother cry. The chance to tell her I didn't mean it has gone. My vocabulary was too young to speak the life I wanted to be living. I have more terms now than I did then.

I have never promised much to anyone. I don't trust myself to say it right.

One day I'll tell you the testament of my scars, how they're a map across my body, connecting the past to the present to the future.

I feel better than I used to. I hear messages on the wind and it makes me feel like I'm part of something greater than my history. It's why I started walking in the woods so much. To hear, to listen. To know something beyond what's been in front of me all along.

The Swiftly Changing Moon

I draw roses across my arm. Declare it a spell of seasons and soil.
Bewitch every hour with tepid reason. The sorcery of a promise
untouched.

I'm finding it hard to hold on. Every vow has gone ragged.
I'm sewing the flesh of each day together, with bleeding hangnails.
When I sleep, I dream my teeth are breaking. My throat fills with
the sound of blue and yellow.

Magic does not work here anymore. I gave it back to the swiftly
changing moon three weeks ago. She took it hungrily, pressing her
lips against the roof of the house for more.

Yesterday I went to the cemetery. Dug at the grave of the first
woman buried there. When the hole was deep enough to cover
my hands, I sank my fists in. The land swelled to fill the space up
to my wrists. The earth always knows what to do. I let myself be
held there.

I started to sing a song that had never before moved through me.
My effort broke against unfamiliar refrains, uneven notes. Still, I
sang louder, defiant and ugly. The sky was overcast. I knelt at that
grave for hours.

In the morning, I woke with a bed full of twigs. In the kitchen,
every cupboard was open. In the mirror, I saw myself as a seven-
day hag. In the shadow beneath my eyes, every dawn. Inside me a
book, sung into being.

How do we know when something has been revealed during sleep?
I remember, I remember, until I don't.

There's a slow morphing shadow marking time across the room. It confides in me that there's more here that I'm meant to know.

I want to consider an invitation to sing through a new grave. What am I giving of myself when I sink into the landscapes of the past and what kind of company is this to keep?

The communion of remembrance is a soft storm brewing within.

Glamour Spell

Girl, you better be ready to see that fallen branches turn to bones every winter. The terrain breaks its spine each season and only I know the songs that bring Her back to life.

Do you want me to sing them to you?

Do you want me to teach you how to see what I see?

Prepare accordingly. The way you're looking at me right now, I don't know that you are. I've read the poetry in your diary. You say you want to control the moon. What kind of magic can you expect to be if you're not willing to walk into the woods at night?

You think it's enough to light a candle once in a while, paint your eyes thick with black and enjoy it whenever someone says you seem *mysterious*.

You think you know me because we made out at that party last weekend. You said you like how I hold your hand, the strength you feel when I touch your skin.

This is my glamour: as soon as you think you know me, I change.

I burn prophecy over open flames and lick the smoke. When I speak, it's through other states. My vocal cords stretch around tidings of chance and hazard. I stretch to fit a stale wind that whooshes from my chest. I channel the part of myself you pretend isn't there.

I show you the secrets of birds and knives, and how to reveal something you have hidden from yourself. I can show you how to regain what's been lost.

But first, we must make the lights go out just by thinking about it. I did it once before and no one knew it was me.

Ready?

Concentrate. When you need to clear your mind, look right here at me. My lips will show you what to do next.

A Low Branch Grazes Your Hair

Why is it that when we
channel nature for its poetry,
we expect it to speak only of landscapes?

Why shouldn't it tell us
of its own death,
the lyrics of lost love.

What if the sound of waves
is the ocean's way of mourning
the lives taken by its depths?

What if our waters are actually
the tears of the Earth's past lives?

Maybe nature is trying to teach us something,
the way it pulls us back to its beaches,
its lakes lapping at our ankles in a language
we've forgotten how to understand.

And when you trip over a root or
feel a low branch graze your hair
it's not an accident, but an act of attention,
everything alive and saying, *Here, I'm here.*

The Earth Spoke and I Listened

I was always waiting for something to happen. I never knew what, so I decided to become something other than what I was.

For a while I shaped myself like a hawk. It opened me to a new question: what is the intention of a feather when it separates itself from the bird?

I let Calliope use me and became a tune. I broke myself trying to dance for you. What did you see in me then?

The earth spoke and I listened. The size of winter didn't fit me anymore, so I went searching for invisible rivers. They run beneath the roads around here. If you put your ear to the ground, you can hear them, singing. Sometimes I dream of drinking from them and wake with a mouth full of diamonds. I always forget how bright the sun gets at this time of year.

Pulling out a root is different than plucking at a leaf. What grows in the descent of autumn is your companion in the ascent of winter.

Next I will become something of tenderness and spring, pushing the rhythm of my joints toward warming soil, vibrant waters.

Everything follows the light no matter how badly you want to stay in the dark.

Pallid Flowers

Soft light of the late winter graces my hand as
an amber word grips my focus. I'm quiet as you
speak of imaginary things.
You believe so much in the importance
of potential. Thread the narrative with wisps
of reality. My jaw tightens. I struggle to swallow.

I'm wearing my defensiveness,
stockings with a run down the back.

The sun catches the scar around your lip, a recollection
that still embarrasses us both. The constant catastrophe
of your persona, I should've known from the start.

The first time we took a cab together you yelled
at the driver when you thought he was taking the long way.
I know the ways you try to scam us, you'd said.
Even though you were wrong, lost
in the north end of town, streets more familiar to me,
I was the one to apologize.

A violet breeze teases the curtains, a thought
I keep repeating. Every morning I grab for it,
try to hold it throughout the day. It's really just a
photograph that comes to me, a snapshot yet to be
taken. Of me, alone. I'm wearing a flowered dress—
pallid fabric and loose straps. A bouquet of orchids
is draped across my arms, coral lipstick popping on a
slight smile. An image of a day that has yet to happen.
A future self I can still become.

Green Goddess

Soft light through the window.
You held my hand and sang of pennyroyal.
The snow had just fallen.
You told me you were tired.
We both were.
Everything important to me
has always been imaginary.

Green goddess, you exorcised this fantasy
lodged between my eyes.
I used to walk in the middle of the road and now
I can't contemplate the last time I was alone.

Helios

Look: this is where the sun broke apart after you tried to pull it down from the sky.

Show me your hands: red and tender, palms the colour of a scream. Now you know what fire feels like. Close your eyes: stare directly at the light and see too much at once. Morning brings the hidden to its death. You never look at me first thing, always wait for the day to be put together before we can speak.

Watch: the sun has gone out, every piece down to ash. What will you see now that it can no longer come between us?

Is this perfection, to blind the day, to see only what you want?

Presence at the Lake

I nested three secrets between the cracks in the floorboards.

The first secret was born on the day we got lost on the east side
of town. We had gone to see a band in the basement of a bar. You
spent your last twenty dollars on beer. Rent was due in three days.

Two girls were standing in front of us at the show. I complimented
one of them on her necklace. Later, waiting for a bus that would
take us in the wrong direction, you pulled her necklace out of your
pocket.

The second secret was the haunting you'd seen along the lake.
How the dead hid beneath the rocks, eyes wide.

For weeks after, you barely left home. When you did, we walked
the same few blocks nearby. I would boil water for your tea, the
leaves loose in the cups. You said you didn't like what you saw in
them.

Do you want to drink something else? I always asked.

No, you said. You liked the way the steam melted against your face.

Mint opened the ways of our expressions. Plants remember
everything. You feed on them and they will eventually feed on you.

The third secret is the one that was left on the tips of our tongues,
shared with us by the life of leaves that once stretched toward the
sun.

What kind of fortune do you think I can tell you with a knowing
like that?

I felt the bones of old petals torn down by storms and worn by rain and sand.

You tasted ciphers spoken over chipped mugs through a voice that was not your own. An initiation we didn't anticipate.

Melt

We won't meet where the light gets in.
Instead, we'll come to each other
under old mud and the ache of time.

I dug up your bones while I was looking for the notions I don't yet
have. Out of the marrow crawled twelve tiny beasts, each with
dark, blinking eyes. Their hungry mouths nipped at the tips of my
fingers and felt their way over inedible surfaces, willing to suck up
whatever they could.

Even a rock. Even a safety pin.

I can't say I'm surprised. You, too, were always more voracious
than cautious. Satiation more important than consequence.

I lost sight of every creature. They crawled behind the baseboards
and into the cupboards.

I didn't have the energy to chase after them. Part of me curious as
to what would happen if I let them stay.

I talk to them now.

Sometimes, they titter at my confessions. Certain honesties,
especially. The dirtier the better. They scratch at the walls asking
for more.

Later, I make black tea and drink it while it's too hot. Burn my
mouth in a cleanse of stories.

Last night I thought I saw your reflection in the back window: baby blue shirt, hair to your collar. The smile you used to have when you were pretending not to be angry. I have been waiting for a new you to write about.

I eat stale cookies off a dirty plate and swallow milk from the carton. The beasts rush toward the crumbs at my feet.

Their chewing is deeply wet, cratered with sighs. Breaking silence.

The Becoming

Set your bare feet on the grass.
Open your awareness. Stay ready to receive.
Your eyes will find the bend of the globe
on which all matters of the future rest.
Predictions hover in the eventide.
Trust in your sight even when your mind
can't keep up.

Wait for the corners of the world to twitch.
Look at how gravity bows to hold you.

You are an open window,
a breeze on the curtains.

Your larynx, an envelope waiting
for a letter to fulfill its purpose.
What missive might you receive?

Let a verse come to mind.
Let another follow. And again.
Pay attention to the lesson
that flows within you.

The Self

Call to the woman who sleeps
between the roots of trees,
who rolls beneath your feet
when you tread on her territory.

(*Mater Daemonicus, I implore you!*)

Leave three coins on a dirt path
and purse your lips
in remorse over a past mistake.
Flex your fingers in defiance of
what you once were.

Call now to the person you might have become
if you'd made other decisions.
What do you see when you watch
yourself from afar?

(*Spiritus Infernali, I implore you!*)

Pull up a weak plant hard
enough to hear the roots
tear from the soil. Cradle this
creature in the crook of your arm.
Ask for its forgiveness.

(Waiting for an answer is the same as
waiting for a spell to work.)

Later, pour a cup of hot water. With honey.
Let its steam rise,
warmth against your lips, cheeks.
Look at your reflection in the water.

(*I invoke thee!*)

The Healing

Visualize you're in a movie
projected across a wide
beige wall.

Act One:

You meet three women
with long hair who teach you
how to dance barefoot in a shallow creek.

Act Two:

Zoom out. Bird's-eye view of
the place you're in. You see it as a chart,
the space shaped like a dragon curled
in sleep.

Act Three:

You're led to a burn that never goes out.
You're told to release three wishes you
no longer care to cultivate.
As you throw them into the fire,
a black dog barks in the distance.

Now, imagine yourself as a ghost
swimming upstream. Somewhere
this image is real.

Taste yourself. Old herbs once passed through
the bodies of your ancestors.
What would they nourish for you?

Maybe the flavour that lingers around your palate
is a remnant of all that was eaten before.
The sustenance of the many who had to exist in order
for you to be here now.

Watch the horizon line at dusk for
the moment the axis shifts.
Somewhere, a sleeping dragon
slips its tail between its teeth.

Inside Every Dream, a Raging Sea

How will I know when it's time to return home?

I'm gathering the Witchery of my ancestors and every corpse
is a tidal poem that threatens to take me under.
How many bridges I've crossed that fell out from beneath me.
My feet, bruised. My blood, buried in shallow mounds.

How will I know when it's time to call myself whole again?

The energy of the land is coming to collect me. I can feel it. Its
grip the sinew of roses and dust, the decay of ambition left in the
bottom of an old drawer.

How will I know when it's time to return home?

Somewhere, my name is being spoken over a candle. Somewhere,
my mother's ghost rocks my childhood in a cradle. Somewhere,
I'm waiting to save myself. Somewhere, I am the legend of a half-
kept promise.

How will I know when it's time to call myself whole again?

I've fallen in love with the sound of wind through the trees, the
force of a thousand songs hummed at once. Here, I let it knock me
on all fours, again and again. I let it keep me there, even though I
may never rise again.

How will I know when it's time to come home?

I've been changed by the strange games they play in these parts. Benedictions have been spoken over me that tied me in charms. Sometimes, I touch wood and it rots away within days. I don't trust my past.

How will I know when it's time to call myself whole again?

I'm choosing a name for myself that only I will know. The hope of sunrise and the smell of rain on rock. Inside every dream, a raging sea.

How will I know when it's time to come home again?

I've been grabbing at every map I find. I'm painting my life the texture of purple and turquoise. I'm seeing the change of light in the sky and I'm waiting, waiting. My legs are tired. My head reels. But still, I move.

Plant Flowers in My Place When I Am Gone

Bless me:
I put three ashen stones across the threshold like you asked,
slept with two more beneath my pillow.

Have mercy on my body.
It's not as strong as it looks and
recoils when lightly touched.
Too many hard stories recorded
across my skin, moments broken
over my softest bones.

Forgive the confusions I've made.
I cut deeper than planned.
Phases I grew out of, yes,
but the regrets age with me.

I do things differently than before and
still somehow end up the same. Bare feet
on cold ground, back aching through
all I hold on to.

Seal the pact.
Plant flowers in my place when I am gone.
Their petals will open in the ways I always wanted to.

The Acceptance

Wake just before sunrise.
Lean against a mirror.
Watch your reflection,
the dawn of a witness.
Hold your lips to the glass.
Breathe. Fog your reflection.
Keep an image of yourself
in childhood sharp
on the edge of your mind.

Breathe again.
Fog your sense of character this time.
Plant a kernel within yourself
to recall something deeper.
Whisper three words
resonant with the feelings
you want to feel again.
Step away from the mirror.

Lay out three piles of herbs:
Rosemary, star anise, rowan.
To the first pile, state:

I've come looking for a time I once knew well.

To the second:

I've come wanting for a tide to turn in my favour.

To the third:

I've come understanding that you are more than you appear.
As you see me, I see you.

As you see me, I see you.
As you see me, I see myself.

Notes

"Other Half" was previously published in *Partial Zine.*

"Not Everything at Once" was originally published in *PRISM international.*

Earlier versions of "The Becoming," "The Self," "The Healing," and "The Acceptance" appeared in a chapbook called *Now, Imagine Yourself as a Ghost*

Acknowledgements

Many of the poems in this book came as whispers. I barely noticed their transmissions. They arrived from Don Valley trails and East York side streets. They owe their dues to an overly warm high-rise apartment and quiet days spent alone.

Some of these are the last poems I wrote before leaving Toronto and so I will thank the city for its sweet goodbyes.

I am grateful to editor Jennifer LoveGrove for her thoughtful insights into each poem.

I also want to give thanks to copy editor Shannon Whibbs for her careful eye. And thank you to designer Gareth Lind for bringing shape and form to this book.

And of course, thank you to Jay and Hazel and the team at Book*hug for all that you do.

Thank you to Mark Hollis, whose music I listened to almost exclusively during the time of these writings. We didn't know each other but Mark's work has changed me forever. His ideas about creativity and rhythm and sound inspired me greatly as I wrote this book.

Thank you to the spirits of Mum and Dad and of all of those who raised and loved me. You may not be here any longer but I know you visit from time to time. We will see each other again.

And thank you to Kire, always.

About the Author

Liz Worth is a poet, novelist, and non-fiction writer. She is a two-time nominee for the ReLit Award for Poetry for her books *The Truth Is Told Better This Way* and *No Work Finished Here: Rewriting Andy Warhol*. Her first book, *Treat Me Like Dirt*, was the first of its kind to provide an in-depth history of Southern Ontario's first-wave punk movement. Her other works also include *Amphetamine Heart*, *PostApoc*, and *The Mouth Is a Coven*. Her writing has appeared in *Chatelaine*, *FLARE*, *PRISM international*, *The Globe and Mail*, the *Toronto Star*, and *Broken Pencil*, among others. Liz is a professional tarot reader and lives in Hamilton, Ontario.

Colophon

Manufactured as the first edition of
Inside Every Dream, a Raging Sea
by Book*hug Press in the fall of 2024

Edited for the press by Jennifer LoveGrove
Copy-edited by Shannon Whibbs
Proofread by Laurie Siblock
Cover photo: unsplash.com/@AnnieSpratt
Design and typesetting by Gareth Lind, Lind Design
Set in Bookmania

bookhugpress.ca